Making Iron

Marie Hartley and Joan Ingilby

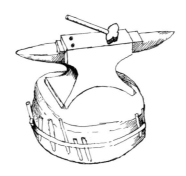

Smith Settle

First published in 1997 by
Smith Settle Ltd
Ilkley Road
Otley
West Yorkshire
LS21 3JP

ISBN 1 85825 081 1

British Library Cataloguing-in-Publication data:
A catalogue record for this book is available from the British Library.

Set in Monotype Plantin

Designed, printed and bound by
SMITH SETTLE
Ilkley Road, Otley, West Yorkshire LS21 3JP

Introduction

The making of ironwork goes back into antiquity, and the former pre-eminence of the smith amongst craftsmen is almost forgotten. Most places had their smith, sometimes two, occasionally three, key figures in local life. Smithwork is composed of two parts usually combined in Dales village smithies — on the one hand the making of tools, gates and agricultural implements, and the fashioning, repairing and sharpening of all manner of household, farming and industrial equipment; and on the other hand the shoeing and care of horses, properly called farrier's work. When new machinery, motor cars and tractors, replacing horses in about 1950, arrived, blacksmiths suffered a mortal blow, and many smithies closed down. But as we shall see, a number survived, engaged in a variety of work.

When, in former centuries, leadmining flourished in the Dales, blacksmiths were employed in the mines. In 1657 the 'Smyth of Maske' (Marske) supplied a bucar (ore crusher) and other things for 2s. They provided nails, hammers, fittings for smelt-mill hearths, and parts for engines when these were installed. In the last century there were four blacksmiths at Gunnerside in Swaledale, a centre for leadmining. One smithy was occupied by the Calvert family, who still have ledgers dating back to the 1840s. One of them, David Calvert (1819–1906), worked part-time for mining companies, but he chiefly presided over a busy smithy.

The Calverts' remarkable archive records the daily work, much of it dealing with horses, and much of it relevant up to the 1950s. In quiet times they were 'on turning shoes' in readiness for local folk who regularly brought in their horses to be shod. 'Removes' were required by some, that is old shoes removed, and new ones made from two. In frosty weather they fitted frost studs in horses' shoes, or took shoes off, sharpened them all over, and replaced them, or fixed a spur, a bar across the toe. Haytime was preceded by the sharpening of shears for clipping sheep, followed by the sale and fitting up of scythes for mowing grass, suiting each customer. Horses, too, were brought in to shoe all at once. David's grandson told us that one haytime he and his son shod fourteen horses working up to midnight. He explained that a set of shoes for a horse on a farm might last a year, but for a horse going regularly on a road a fortnight.

Smiths also co-operated with joiners and stonemasons, well illustrated in the Calvert ledgers. For the former they supplied iron hoops and undertook the hooping of wheels, also iron fittings for carts, and such things as loops for coffin handles. For the masons they provided new mells (hammers), wedges for quarrying, gavelocks (crowbars), pincers, jumpers (borers) and so on, as well as sharpening their tools. Before veterinary surgeons arrived, the smith was relied on to treat sick animals with ointments, even bleeding, and surgical shoes. Every day household and farming equipment was brought in for repairs.

David Calvert had three sons, all of whom became blacksmiths, and one, William, settled at Askrigg in Wensleydale, as innkeeper and blacksmith at the Crown Inn. A relation, Calvert Chapman, in the late 1930s made all the wrought ironwork for our cottage at Askrigg, such as snecks and hinges for large and small doors, and cupboards, a hood for a fireplace, and electric candlelight holders. Calvert had smithies at Askrigg and Bainbridge which both closed when he retired in 1957.

The smithy at Gunnerside is now a museum of blacksmith and lead-mining artefacts, but David's great-great-grandson is a farmer there.

Redolent of the atmosphere of former days, the blacksmith's shop houses an accumulation of tools — flatters, swages, fullers, mandrels, pincers, tongs, hammers — cluttering up every corner, and together with horseshoes hanging on beams. The stone-built forge, often two in the one smithy, dominates, and is large enough to contain a hoop for a wheel. Alongside are the bellows, sometimes two, and once pear-shaped, but now round, and once pumped by a handle with a cow's horn at the end, but now driven by an electric motor. Under the hearth is a slake trough for tempering, and nearby the main feature, the anvil on a wooden base. At Askrigg smithy there was formerly a little swing-seat, and a small anvil fitted into a hole for pointing nails.

A porch alongside or an adjoining building serves as a shoeing shed, and outside are a grindstone, cramps for bending hoops, a wheel stand on which the wheel was screwed down for hooping, and sometimes a slaking trough.

In the 1930s the smith at Grassington, whose premises were then on the right as you entered the market place, remembered the job of shoeing the webbed feet of geese, as flocks were brought down from the North, by driving them through tar and sand. At Redmire in 1823 there were three blacksmiths, no doubt owing to the proximity of Keld Head lead-mines. The last smithy there closed down about 1950, and the smith, William Robinson, recollected shoeing cattle with the beast on its back. A pole was put between their hind legs so that one leg came up, and the animal went down. Cattle have cloven hoofs, so that their shoes consisted of two small plates. Here at Redmire they fashioned plough shares for the farms in mid-Wensleydale with arable land. They also perpetuated a charming custom by giving a 'reckon' (an adjustable hook used to hang pots over an open fire) to newly-married couples. To shoe a fractious horse, J J Tallon of Sedbergh described how a cart rope was placed round a horse's neck fastened to each side, and around the fetlocks of the back legs. A man at either side pulled, drawing in the fetlocks, so that the animal came down.

John Holmes of Austwick and Clapham served five years' apprenticeship for two shillings a week, and aged seventy in 1967, had worked for fifty-seven years. At haytime sharpening scythes by candlelight, they were often up until 11pm. 'You have to be born to it.' In frosty weather the Hodgsons of Settle once sharpened the shoes of twenty-eight horses, working until three in the morning, and the Calverts of Gunnerside sometimes set aside a day for the hooping of six or eight wheels, which was 'a hot hard job'.

At Hawes in 1996 R B Spencer, aged eighty-nine, still worked at the smithy. When he was fifteen, he was apprenticed to John Oswald Dinsdale, working from 8am to 7pm, and starting at eight shillings a week. The first job in the morning was to light the forge fire. In those days there were five forges in three smithies in Hawes. On market days Bob Spencer would shoe ten horses, but 'it was a killer'. One day when we were there, he was sharpening picks for county council men, that involved tempering and judging by the colour through brown, purple and bees-wing to blue, as the tip was hammered and plunged alternately into water. This year he was making hornburns for the marking of sheep. But his nephews are plumbers and central heating engineers.

Middleham in Wensleydale has a resident farrier, John McCormack, engaged in shoeing the valuable racehorses there. He has been in charge of stables for thirty-five years. Visiting each in turn and cold shoeing, he shoes six to eight racehorses in a day, taking three-quarters of an hour for each. Yearlings that come in for their first shoeing are easily alarmed, but he has only had three mishaps.

At Settle and Malham the smithies are in active use, since 1991 run by a family group. John Clements works at Malham, and his son David and daughter-in-law Rachel at Settle, all engaged in ornamental wrought-ironwork. David trained in design at college at Hull, and Rachel took up this work when she saw how much her husband enjoyed it. She has been awarded her Forgework Certificate at the end of the New Entrants Blacksmith Course at college in Salisbury, where she was the only woman, and has several certificates, some for her competence from the Worshipful Company of Blacksmiths. They use special tools — scroll wrenches, forks, crimp and leaf tools — for bending and moulding. The Clements are all highly skilled, and are kept very busy making anything from fire irons to gates.

New technology has brought change to smith work. Horseshoes and nails used to be made in the local smithy, and are now usually bought in. Cold shoeing not hot shoeing is general, and mild steel is used instead of iron. Electricity in harnessed to drills, grinders, oxy-acetylene equipment, fans for forges and so on, thus lightening work for the smith.

Photographic Acknowledgements

We wish to thank Mr F D Woodall for the photograph on page 14 (also used on the cover); J McCormack for that on page 43; and P Sharp for those on pages 44-47.

The blacksmith's shop for Beldi Hill leadmine near Keld, Swaledale. Note Crackpot Hall down below on the left. (1950s.)

David Calvert
(1819–1906),
blacksmith of
Gunnerside, and
member of a
family of black-
smiths. He is
wearing a paper
hat

David Calvert junior, shoeing a horse at Gunnerside smithy in the 1890s.
Old David is seen on the left. Note the typical blacksmith's shoeing box.

William and David Calvert sharpening a
scythe blade on a grindstone (1880s).

David's son William Calvert at Askrigg smithy behind the Crown Inn, early this century, about to shoe Old Bowly.

Gunnerside smithy in the 1950s, with William Calvert, Old David's grandson, on the right.

The smithy at Redmire (date unknown). The blacksmith makes a horseshoe on the anvil, and his assistant has his left hand on the handle to pump the bellows. Note the swage block, a pile of horseshoes and the hoop for a wheel.

Shoeing a horse at Kettlewell smithy.
This is now a gift shop for tourists.

Bob Spencer shoeing a Dales pony at Hawes smithy in the 1930s. There were then two smithies alongside each other. Note the backcan on the right.

Bob Spencer starting to shoe a pony in the 1950s, by heating a shoe in the fire on the hearth. He is an expert on shoes of all shapes and sizes, and in the Second World War made shoes to be sent to Italy for mules.

Turning the heel of the shoe. Note the divided leather apron suited to the holding of a horse's foot.

Note the slaking trough for tempering under the hearth on
the bottom right. The flat stone by his left hand has been
hollowed over the years by rubbing to sharpen chisels.

The red-hot shoe
is held by tongs.
Repeated heatings
and hammerings
shape the shoe to
fit the horse's foot.

Hammering the shoe to make it round on the pike end of the anvil.

Smoothing the hoof with a rasp preparatory to shoeing, after trimming with the pareing knife which rests on top of the shoeing box. Note the shoe hanging ready to be put on.

After fitting the shoe on, nailing it with the shoeing hammer, taking care to point the nails outwards and upwards to avoid the sensitive part of the hoof.

With the shoeing hammer which has a claw end, the protruding points of the nails are clinched (bent over) to secure the shoe.

Fixing a blade on to a scythe: first the heel of the blade is heated, and
burnt into place on the handle; then the ring holds the blade firm.

The smith attends to a customer, Frank Outhwaite, to fit up a scythe. The distance between the handles should be the length of the forearm.

Testing the angle of the scythe blade to the handle. Notice the grass nail joining the handle and blade.

Bob Spencer filing initials on a hornburn. These used to be made of iron, but now mild steel is used. This is a skilled job. (1996)

He shows several that he has made. Most have two initials of the farmer or the farm. Hornburns are made red-hot and the initials burnt on to the horn of a sheep.

Edgar Armstrong of Arncliffe, Littondale, shoeing a horse at Malham smithy. He uses a stand to support a front leg.

Edgar Armstrong, blacksmith at Arncliffe,
Littondale, drills holes for screws to attach
iron shoes to the runners of a wooden sledge,
which is upside-down. It is a good example of
co-operation between smith and joiner.

John Holmes, blacksmith at Clapham and Austwick, finishing making a hornburn. He punches a hole to show which way up the tool should be held.

He tries it out on a wooden door. This smithy is now closed.

W J Hodgson in Dent smithy. A typical corner of a smithy, with horseshoes hanging from a beam and many tools — pincers and tongs at hand, a vice near his elbow and the anvil bottom right. This smithy still functions, repairing agricultural implements.

J H Tallon and his assistant acting as striker using a sledgehammer to make a horseshoe at Sedbergh smithy in the 1960s. The smithy closed about 1990.

J H Tallon and his father J J Tallon starting to hoop a wheel. John Tallon measures the circumference of the wheel with the traveller, at Barbon smithy near Sedbergh.

He now measures the inner circumference of the iron hoop with the traveller, by means of chalk marks and counting the number of rotations.

Heating the hoop on the hearth for piecing.

Piecing the hoop.

Lifting with iron tyre-dogs the red-hot hoop, which has been heated on a circle of burning logs, to place on the wheel screwed down on the tyreing platform.

Slaking the hoop so that it contracts and tightens.

A wheel in a trough, fed by a small stream, for slaking at Gunnerside, held by blacksmith Jim Calvert, great-grandson of David Calvert, and joiner Percy Calvert.

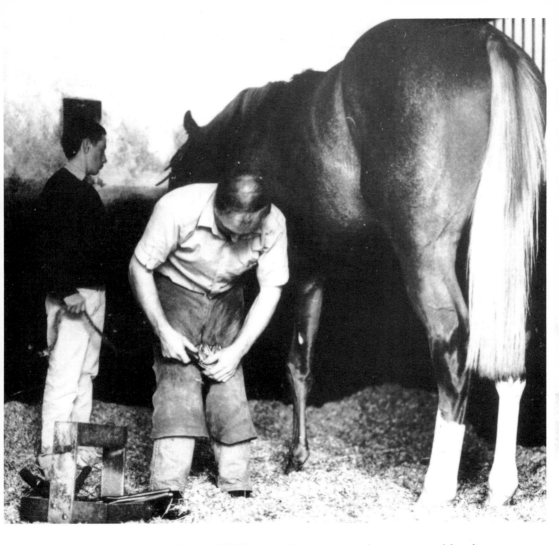

John McCormack, farrier at Middleham, shoeing a racehorse at a stables there.

John Clements
working at Malham
smithy, making a
scroll for a gate for
the churchyard at
Coniston Cold. He
uses both a bending
and a hand fork on
the anvil to adjust the
curve of the scroll.

David Clements at
Settle smithy,
repairing a broken
hinge-pin for a
wrought-iron gate at
Giggleswick School.
He is using an
electric welder.

Rachel Clements at Settle smithy. She is cleaning up an acanthus leaf for a gate — a test piece worked at college in Salisbury, where she completed an apprenticeship course in forgework run by the Rural Development Commission.

John and David Clements at Settle smithy. They are forging a tenon on a gate. This is heavy iron, and needs a striker to wield a large hammer, while the smith holds the work and the former in place — a four-handed job.